A ROYAL MAKEOVER

Foreword by Pastor Gail Roberts-House &
Pastor Danielle Murphy

SHANICKA VAIL HOUSE

Printed in the United States of America

ISBN: 0692418954
ISBN-13: 978-0692418956

DEDICATION

There is a freedom to "be ME" that I experience

each time I complete this 30 day journey! And

because I pray that you would experience it too,

this book is dedicated to "U"!

...the NEW (more be.Utee-ful) YOU!

"Behold, I will do a new thing, Now it shall spring forth;
Shall you not know it?..." (Isaiah 43:19 NKJV)

FOREWORD

by Pastor Gail Roberts-House
Senior Pastor
Open Door Full Gospel Baptist Church
Hampton, Virginia

The chronicles of life sometimes create mental cell blocks that tend to lock us within gates of bondage. Life happens...things change...people change...but GOD remains our constant and ultimate change agent! How do we escape in order to find who we really are? What can we do to break the chains of exasperation, discontent, and just stuff in general? Our Savior, the ultimate craftsman and potter, needs to make some adjustments; and in most cases needs to create a new mold from the clay. Our old ways need to be put in the past. We should put them behind us, like old clothes to be given away, because they no longer 'fit' into what God has predestined for our lives. We must get a new wardrobe, head in a new direction and allow the transformation that only the Holy Spirit can provide.

Shanicka Vail-House has heard God's voice in guiding her pen to create the prescriptive pages in this book, not only for you to examine where you are, but to make you over that you might become the person you are ordained by God. I was particularly impressed by her down-to-earth style and personal approach. As a young author, this book is seasoned, steeped and saturated in such a way that hearts will be touched and lives changed.

This 30 day Makeover provides a strategic plan for the reader's progressive and successful end. She has identified scripture passages to accompany each of the 30 days as you take this journey. This creates a foundational bridge that allows you to identify yourself and take a spiritual walk in the word. Periodically, you will be requested to document your route as you articulate your goals and next steps. If you walk through these pages with purpose, you will find that NEW you when you arrive at the finish line. Be sure to make significant notes on your journey so that each step creates a new path for where God is directing you. You will begin to see that, what had seemed to be a never ending tunnel of darkness, was really the beginning of your new pathway to greatness. Shanicka's formula equates it like this: **Want + Work = WIN!**

A Royal Makeover provides direction, guidance, insight and encouragement that will allow you to reach the full capacity of your God ordained potential. Take pleasure in reading this book as you journey to a new dimension of spiritual growth.

FOREWORD

by Pastor Danielle Murphy
dReam Center Church of Atlanta
Atlanta, Georgia

I believe God assigns Kingdom voices to speak to a certain group of people regarding particular topics or issues. In order for their voice to be heard, they must submit to God's process which sharpens the sound they possess to be distinctly heard.

I believe that my daughter, *Shanicka Vail-House*, is one of those voices. Over the past nine years, I have been blessed to witness her submit to the plan of God and be molded as an instrument prepared to speak to those who will hear God's message through her.

This awesome work, *"A Royal Makeover"*, will take its readers on a journey of self-discovery. It's origin is not cerebral as it is penned directly from the heart of its author. Shanicka takes you on a path that she first travelled. She unselfishly shares with the readers the valuable nuggets given to her directly from the mouth of God.

It is my prayer that, as you read this tool, you too, like Shanicka will be "Royally" transformed to *be.U* and step into your purpose and destiny!

DAY ONE

"What Do U See?"
Today's Scripture: Jeremiah 1 (Focus: v. 5)

In the first book of Jeremiah, The Lord spoke to Jeremiah, telling him that before he was ever formed in his mother's womb, He knew him. The Lord told Jeremiah that before he was born, He sanctified him, and ordained him a prophet to the nations. This is the way God saw Jeremiah; this is what He had already known about him. BUT, Jeremiah did not see himself the way that The Lord saw him and he responded to God saying, "Ah, Lord God! Behold, I cannot speak, for I am a youth."

This conversation between God and Jeremiah is pretty funny if you pay close attention. The whole point of God speaking to Jeremiah was to get him to understand the plan that was carved out of eternity's hand for him. God needed him to see that there was a calling on his life to speak to the nations. But, what does Jeremiah do? He uses his mouth (the thing needed to speak) and his age to discredit his assignment in the world. That's what makes this a funny irony -- that he would tell God what he couldn't do while using the very instrument that correlates with his assignment. Why did he do this? I wasn't there and I don't know what his thought process was at the time, but I can almost guarantee that he did this because he didn't see what God saw. So many of us are like Jeremiah when we learn what it is God wants us to do.

What has The Lord said about you that you don't yet believe? That you don't see when you look at or think of yourself? Perhaps it is hard for you to believe what GOD says about you, and who He says that you are, because you have believed all of the wrong things that PEOPLE have said about you; or maybe you are so set in what you have been thinking and saying about yourself that you don't know how to move away from it just yet.

After Jeremiah's response, The Lord corrected him, purposed him, instructed him, touched him, AND questioned him saying, "Jeremiah, what do you see?" What a life-defining moment this must have been for Jeremiah....because God was giving him the opportunity to answer a question he probably never asked himself prior to this encounter. He didn't ask because He was clueless concerning Jeremiah's identity, but rather because He desired for Jeremiah to comprehend that regardless of what He saw, he needed to ultimately see what was true about this purpose and assignment -- and that could not happen independent of this question being asked.

Just like Jeremiah, this same question has been proposed and we must answer it. Not tomorrow but today. You are too great to be living without an awareness of who you really are. I know that you are still in your "youth" but you are destined for greatness. Your assignment in the earth is great and the potential you have to change the world with your peculiarities is limitless. The only thing that can stop you is your inability to see what God sees when He stares at you.

Go look in the mirror, and in your notes write down what you see when you view yourself in the mirror. This may become VERY emotional for you, but don't back away. Let your heart break if it must. Allow yourself to be vulnerable and open so that you can discover the "U" that you may have tried to prevent from fully emerging, never knew existed, or always had a difficult time accepting because you didn't believe that anyone would "get you" or love that version of who you are. Whatever you see in the mirror, whatever you feel while standing there, and whatever thoughts consume your mind in that moment -- write it all down.

I know stepping out on this type of faith is scary because you can't really tell what is on the other side of your bravery. I get it. I understand. The truth, however, is that you don't have to do this in your own strength; you don't have to do this without God. To be quite honest with you, He has every intention of being present the entire time. Over these next 30 days, expect to receive "a touch from God" that will trigger a shift in your vision and cause you to see yourself the way that He sees you. Remember, He knows THE REAL "U"! It's time for you to discover THE REAL "U", too!

DAY TWO

"What Do U Hear?"
Today's Scripture: Luke 10 (Focus: v.41-42)

Yesterday, we gave our focus to the importance of seeing what God sees as it relates to our life, our purpose, and our assignments. While that is very vital, what good is seeing if it's not accompanied by hearing? We have to hear as much as we see. Both of these functions must coexist if we are going to be successful at achieving our royal makeovers, and doing life once the makeover has been obtained.

In Luke 10, the sisters, Mary and Martha, are visited by Jesus. Martha wanted to make sure that the home was ready to host a guest of Jesus' magnitude so, as many of us would, she busied herself serving. I mean, Jesus is coming over to the house, so you'd better make sure everything is on point upon His arrival, right? Well, that was Martha's agenda. Her sister on the other hand, sat at Jesus' feet and did what Martha was too busy to do -- she heard His word. Martha, annoyed at her sister's lack of service, basically told on her for not helping. To this, Jesus essentially said to Martha that she was worried about the wrong thing at that moment. Martha was busy "working" when she needed to, like Mary, be busy "listening". It's not that she was wrong for cleaning and wanting to welcome Jesus into a tidy environment. The real issue was that she had the right motive at the wrong time.

Martha is very much like the average person that finds themselves wrapped up in something that seems important but is a distraction from what really matters at that time. Whenever being busy impedes your hearing Jesus, there's an issue that must be rectified immediately because everything about living as the Royal U will require that you seek and hear from Jesus. Now, of course there are some things that you cannot get out of doing. I'm not recommending that you neglect your responsibilities, whatever they might be; however, I do intend to help you understand that it's not wise to run around trying to get a *"To Do List"* complete and miss Jesus' voice in the process. The simple fact is, a visit from Jesus matters more than the mundane things -- and even those things that are rightfully significant.

Did you stop to hear from God today? Before you got your day started, did you take a moment to listen?

I know... you, just like Martha, have a lot of things to do. You're busy and everything needs your attention. You have deadlines. You have homework. You have church stuff. You have extracurricular "outside of the home" obligations. BUT - don't get so caught up in "work" that you forget your "assignment".

What is your level of intentionality about hearing the voice of God? Unless that level is high, you will have more missed moments than divine encounters of hearing the one voice that holds your world together. It isn't my goal to scare you, but that is a very detrimental reality to live in.

I want to challenge you to remove whatever stands in the way of you hearing from God. Doing this may mean you will have to remove some things and rearrange others, but whatever you do, do not be Martha running around doing this and that while Jesus is waiting for you to find a seat at His feet so He can speak into and over you.

For the remainder of these 30 days, and every day thereafter, listen for the still small voice. Purpose to hear what God wants for and from you. Listen to know what He says ABOUT you and hear the instructions for what you must do...and write it all down so that what you heard you can now see and carry to completion.

<u>DAY THREE</u>

"What Are U Saying?"
Today's Scripture: Mark 11 (Focus: v.23)

In Mark 11 Jesus was with the disciples leaving Bethany. He was hungry, saw a fig tree with leaves in the distance, and went up to the tree to see if He could find something on it. But, guess what? There was NOTHING BUT LEAVES!!

Now, put yourself in Jesus' shoes for a moment. Imagine that you're driving, you've actually been driving for hours, and you're hungry! All of a sudden, you see some "golden arches". Excited, you swing by the drive-thru, order, grab your bag, and when you look inside - IT'S EMPTY!! Not a good look, is it? Well, when Jesus saw that this tree had no fruit, He said to it, "Let no one eat fruit from you ever again." His disciples heard it, and they continued on their journey.

As Jesus and the disciples were returning from their journey they had to pass by this same tree again, and this time the tree looked nothing like the day before. The tree had dried up from the roots, at HIS WORD!! What a difference one day---well, one word---can make! Jesus spoke to His disciples saying, "For assuredly, I say to you, whoever says to this mountain, 'Be removed and be cast into the sea,' and does not doubt in his heart, but believes that those things he says will be done, he will have whatever he says."

What a powerful demonstration of the weight that words have. Yesterday, Jesus spoke to the tree. Today in passing with his disciples, He sees what He said the day before in living color. It took a few words spoken with full belief to create a reality for tomorrow. I know what you're probably thinking, "...but it doesn't always happen that QUICK" or "my words don't have the same power as Jesus'". To that I say, it's not about how quickly it happens.

It may happen instantly or it may very well happen gradually; however, you only need to say what you want to see and believe that if you tell the mountain to move, it will. Secondly, we don't have the same power in words as Jesus does, but we have authority to speak.

What are you saying about what is happening in your life? Are you speaking what you see? Or, are you speaking what you believe?

Your words are POWERFUL! They are life and death; they are the difference between one reality and the next. For most of us, our mountains are still standing tall, not because they're too great to be removed, but because we're either too doubtful or too unconcerned to speak to them. On this journey, the key to change will oftentimes be your words. Nothing will change just because you want it it to. Things will change because you've found enough faith to unlock possibilities with your words.

At all times, be mindful of what you say. Unsure of what to say? Ask yourself these questions and answer them honestly:

- **What do I want to see?**

- **What "mountains" are here that need to be removed?**

- **What "trees" are standing but not producing fruit?**

From your answers to these questions, create daily declarations to match each of them. Also, in your notes, write down the promises and words that have been spoken over your life, write down scriptures from the Bible that speak to your situation(s), and begin to declare ALOUD (where your circumstances can hear) the TRUTH over your FACTS! Devote to doing this daily and watch how your declarations come alive.

DAY FOUR

"Where Are U Going?"
Today's Scripture: Habakkuk 2 (Focus: v.2)

Life absolutely needs a direction. There has to be a very clear map, blueprint, and outline that is specifically in place to help you get from point A to point B, from vision to completion, from start to finish. Whenever your life lacks direction, your feet wanders aimlessly and you will find yourself on a lot of paths that were never meant to be traveled on your journey. That said, where are you going? Now that you've started pondering the answer to that, here's another question: where are the people affiliated with your vision going?

Habakkuk, the prophet, had been asking The Lord questions - and what we have in the second chapter is an answer to questions Habakkuk posed in Chapter 1. It is written, "the Lord answered him saying, 'Write the vision and make it plain on tablets. That he may run who reads it.'" (v.2). Let's hit PAUSE for a brief moment to peel back two layers from this focus verse.

Layer 1: Habakkuk was instructed to write the vision and make it plain. This wasn't a task being given without good reason behind it. He was told to do this because if the vision remained in his mind and never made it to paper, the likelihood of him making good on it was slim. Why? We are more prone to achieve our goals when they become clear and concise to us. By writing something down, especially your visions/goals, it becomes a little more real to you and since you can see it in word form, it's no longer just a "good idea". A vision on paper becomes plain and seems possible but a vision never written down is just another thought in your mind.

Layer 2: The second clause of this focus verse says "that he may run who reads it". This statement clearly defines the system that should be followed for making something come of the vision you have. The system is simple: one person writes the vision and another person(s) reads what has been written and runs with it. Following this system enforces teamwork and eliminates the mindset so many visionaries have and that is, "I can do it all alone". Yes, you might be very capable and competent but every vision needs assistance. So, even if you can do it all alone (most times, you won't since God usually gives us visions that are way bigger than we are), you shouldn't because just like God intended for someone to run with Habakkuk's vision, He intends the same for yours.

Okay, let's hit PLAY and continue where we left off. Have you ever been instructed to go somewhere you've never been before, and all you have to guide you is someone's written instructions? How important is it that those instructions make sense to you? How much SLOWER do you move on your way there when the instructions aren't "plain"? You need it to be clear so you can be effective, right? Well, think about that in relation to the vision that God has given to you, and the people He's assigned/assigning to help you carry it out. Just like you, they will need very clear and "plain" directives.

Most assistants don't mind going as long as they have what they need to get there. A person is more willing to do the work when they have enough to start with. As the person responsible for communicating the vision God gave you to others, keep this in mind at all times: you have to talk to people in THEIR language. It's expected for YOU to "get it" because the vision belongs to you. Your team has to learn it so you have to teach on their level. As time progresses, their tenure with you will teach them how to think, operate, and execute like you, but in the beginning stages, be prepared to teach your assistants how to assist you. Never just send them; take time to tell them (verbally or written) where to go. This is what it means to "make it plain" so that others can run with it.

What has the Lord given you a passion and desire for?

What VISION has He given to you?

Do you have the desire for something bigger than you currently see?

In your notes, begin to write out those desires...those things that you are passionate about. Write out a plan that incorporates those desires into your life, and if some of those things are not areas that you naturally work in - ask for wisdom on how to grow in those areas, AND how to "make your vision plain" so that those who ARE gifted in those areas will be able to read it and help you run with it! God honors a plan...just make sure you leave the necessary room for His plan/agenda/will to be fulfilled.

DAY FIVE

"What Have U Lost?"
Today's Scripture: 1 Samuel 30 (Focus: v.8)

In this passage of scripture David and his men had come to find out that there had been an invasion, their women and children had been taken captive, and their place had been burned with fire. The men were devastated, and who wouldn't be? Even David was greatly distressed; however, he strengthened himself in The Lord. David inquired of The Lord if he should pursue and overtake the troop that had invaded their space and taken their families and their things.

Imagine that you've been at work ALL DAY long. From 9 o'clock in the morning, until 5 o'clock in the evening, you worked tirelessly. Although you're tired, you are smiling as you make your way through the traffic because you are just ready to be at home, relax, and enjoy your family, but when you arrive at home and walk up to your door, it is wide open, all of your belongings are gone, and your family is nowhere to be found. Gut-wrenching, isn't it? There are very few things that are as devastating as this scenario.

For a lot of you reading this, you've had your normalcy disrupted, just as David did, with some of the things that you have lost up to this point. It's one thing to misplace something or lose it on your own accord, but when things begin scattering and leaving due to outside sources, it's no longer just another loss and it's more than just having something gone. In more ways than one, it changes your entire life and if you're anything like me, the question immediately becomes: *HOW DO I GET IT BACK?*

This journey is so much bigger than being made over; it surpasses restoration. This is also a time where you have the right to reclaim everything that was wrongfully taken from you despite the reason it was taken. It doesn't matter if your belongings were stolen because someone envious of you came and burglarized the items within your personal space--your peace, your joy, your job, your sense of self. The only thing that really matters is that you were caught at a time of being busy or unaware and someone/something showed up and left with what they didn't arrive with, and you need everything back.

When a resident calls the police station to report a home invasion, one of the primary questions asked by the operator/officer is: do you know what was taken from you? Though the nature of this question is simple, it's ESSENTIAL to the recovery of what has been lost/stolen. If you don't know what is missing, you don't know what to look for. If you're not able to identity what was taken from you, that indicates that you don't take inventory of your life well enough, or at all. Whenever that's the case, the "enemy" sees your life as an easy target because if YOU don't know what you have, how will you know when it's gone?

What things have you lost while you were out?

Has the enemy plundered and taken your peace, joy,

strength, boldness, self-esteem, dignity, self-worth?

What has gone from being constant to nonexistent?

In your notes today, take inventory of the things that you've lost over time. PLEASE, be careful not to confuse what's been taken by the enemy with the things that God took away from you for your betterment. Some, if not all, of what God has uprooted from your life is not coming back--so don't waste your time trying to fit things from the past in a future that's too big for them. The only things worth recovering are things that complement the future you're headed towards. If it doesn't, let it remain gone. Miss it (whatever it is) if you have to, but remain future-focused.

Now that you are clear on what was removed by God and what was taken by the enemy, gather your list, go to the enemy's camp, and take back everything that he stole from you! **PURSUE, OVERTAKE, and RECOVER ALL!!!**

DAY SIX

"What Issue(s) Do U Have?"
Today's Scripture: 1 Samuel 1 (Focus:: v:2; 10-20)

There was a woman in the Bible by the name of Hannah. Hannah was married to a husband who loved her deeply. He did everything that he could to make Hannah happy, but the one thing that she really wanted, her husband could not give to her. Hannah had no children, but desperately wanted them. Now, Peninnah, the other wife of Hannah's husband, had children and was a constant reminder of Hannah's issue.

Do you know what it's like to be the Hannah of your household, in your circle of friends, at your church? I can bet that most of us have been - or may be - exactly where Hannah was. You know, every day you wake up expecting that God will FINALLY make that miracle happen for YOU, but instead, it happens for everyone else right in front of your face. So, not only are you challenged with celebrating them instead of becoming jealous or angry, but you also have to resuscitate your faith so that it does not fail completely. If you have ever lived this for yourself, you are no stranger to the anguish that Hannah had to endure.

Hannah became a bit bitter, but can you honestly blame her? Even feeling the way that she did, Hannah did not allow her prayers to be suffocated by her bitterness. As disappointed as she might have been, somehow she managed to cling to a mustard seed of faith that kept her in God's presence making supplications. That's a sheer demonstration of faith. And let's be clear, having faith does not eliminate your humanness; instead, it gives you the strength to choose fervor over feelings. Fervor is what keeps you praying when everything about your situation stays the same instead of changing. Hannah never quit praying. She knew exactly who could not only help her with her issue, but teach her how to overcome it. She prayed and petitioned God to help her with her issue, no matter how foolish it made her look. That's another truth to note about faith -- sometimes it makes you look foolish to others and even to yourself. Why? Because although faith is pushing you into prayer, prayer may not produce what you are expecting right away. However, just like Hannah, we have to be so desperate that we continue living by faith without being controlled by what we have not seen yet. She was desperate and desperate times called for desperate measures.

Think of one thing that you really want, and imagine not being able to have it. Now, think that your sister or brother have SEVERAL of the ONE thing that you want, and although you're exposed to it every day, it doesn't make you feel better because it is not yours. Not only is it not yours, but it hurts to look at it because it serves as a constant reminder of YOUR ISSUE. You applied for the job and met every qualification for the position, but instead of you getting it, someone in your immediate circle received it. You needed that financial blessing, not for any selfish reason but to pay an outstanding bill or to fund a vision God trusted you with, but the mailman dropped the check off in your neighbor's mailbox instead of yours. This is such a disappointing space to be in and you truly have to be careful about how you respond because even though you may feel forgotten, it doesn't dismiss that God is looking for you to maintain your trust in Him and be of good cheer.

How do you react to the things that remind you of your issue? How do you cope when someone else is living in the solution to your issue? What becomes of your belief about God when He makes everyone else the miracle but you?

What issues do you have? Are you in denial about them? Have you become "comfortable" with them? Are you content to just live life ignoring the fact that you have issues? Are you denying the fact that there are things in your life that need to be confronted? Can you, WILL y

face you and your pressing issues, and seek God for the

solution(s)?

In your notes write down your issues, the ones that you know you have. But, don't stop there - ask God to show you some issues that aren't necessarily at the forefront, but are affecting areas of your life. This will require you to dig deep, and possibly even require you to stand in front of the mirror again. But do whatever it takes. God can use you, even with your issues...but what is more important, He can also get you over those issues! Today, your charge is pretty simple: CONFRONT and CONQUER!

DAY SEVEN

"Do U Have Faith?"
Today's Scripture: Daniel 3 (Focus: v. 17-18)

In this focus verse, we have Daniel's three friends: Shadrach, Meshach, and Abed-Nego who are pointed out for being "different". There has been a decree in the land that everyone who hears the sound of the horn, flute, lyre, and psaltery, in symphony with all kinds of music, shall fall down and worship the golden image. Shadrach, Meshach, and Abed-Nego decided that they will have NO OTHER god before their God. They went against the grain and took a risk to STAND. Now, the consequence for not bowing was not a delicate one whatsoever. If you chose against bowing, the consequence was to be thrown into the fiery furnace. OUCH! Were the three Hebrew boys moved by this? No. Not even a little bit! They told the king that whether he decided to throw them into the furnace or not, they would not bow because their God would deliver them.

Many would say that this story showed that the 3 Hebrew boys were disrespectful and had no regard for the law, but I beg to differ. To me, this story shows absolute and beautiful devotion to God, not disrespect to the law. It shows that you have to choose Christ over culture and let faith overshadow fear. Furthermore, it shows that standing for God and what you believe in may offend others, and it may even land you in an uncomfortable furnace, however, that is the price tag on being different. When you are different, fitting in is impossible. When you are completely sold out to God, your life doesn't have any vacancies to hold anything that doesn't resemble God.

One of the most admirable details about this story was the concrete faith that they placed in God. With every fiber of their being, they made it very clear that they would not bow because they KNEW that their God would deliver them. In other words, they were saying, "do what you gotta do and my God will do what He has to do". If that is not a bold, radical illustration of unwavering faith, please tell me what is. The definition of faith becomes so real when you read through this story and understand the details. These 3 boys were not going to be sentenced to prison; they were not going to have their license suspended indefinitely, or owe the government taxes. The consequences for their devotion to their God was far more extreme. A fiery furnace was their punishment for refusing to bow down to a god that was not their God, but it did not move them one bit. WOW! It speaks high volumes of your faith in God when you are willing to burn for trusting Him instead of bowing at the expense of betraying Him.

Knowing that God will deliver you gives your faith a boost. However, believing that even if He doesn't deliver you, He's still able to---that is what makes your faith immovable. Many times we would like to use God as some type of "genie"... "I'll rub your bottle (worship You) if

You'll come out and grant my wish. But when we don't receive what we have asked or wished for IMMEDIATELY, we begin to lose trust in the Almighty God. We have to grow to a "praise You if You do OR DON'T" place. Have that immovable faith that says, "either I'll live to tell people of the miracle You performed, or I'll die in Your name".

It's not easy being under pressure of any kind. When you can't see what is on the other side of your decisions, it is really hard to make the one that requires blind faith. In this story, they knew what would be next because they were told what would happen if they chose not to listen to the decree given -- but what happens when you do not know what your "fiery furnace" will be for having faith in your God? It may not occur daily, but at different intervals of your journey, you will definitely find yourself at a breaking point. Our breaking points only crush us when our faith lacks the strength to sustain us. Just imagine how differently this story could have panned out if they did not believe that deliverance would happen for them. Honestly, some of you may not need to use their story to find this true because you can recall a time when you slipped up and fell from your faith.

What "heated" situation(s) are you facing right now? What is the enemy trying to get you to bow to? Will you "stand" in faith believing that God will deliver?

In your notes write down some things in your life that would seek to break you down and make you bend, and then ask God to give you strength building exercises to stand in spite of those heavy-weighted circumstances. Even if there are people in your life who are falling prey to things you know you can't be a part of, and you need to know how to break away - ask God for the "how to". When you're a little unsure, know that HE ALWAYS has the answers. STAND UP and STAND OUT!! God's got you covered!!

DAY EIGHT

"What Are U Holding On To?"
Today's Scripture: Acts 9 (Focus: v.18)

In this passage of scripture, God is sending Ananias to "Straight Street" to an enemy, as far as he knows, to bring healing to him. Ananias only knew bad about Saul, and the bad was validated by what Saul's actions had been in the past. Although we are made aware of Saul's violent past, we can see documented all throughout the scriptures the massive amount of work that PAUL (formerly Saul) did for the Kingdom.

Question: what if Ananias refused to go against what he "knew" about Saul, and chose not to follow God's instructions? Can you imagine Paul's conversion never happening? Or, can you imagine the Bible without Paul's portion ever being written? All in all, we know that if Ananias hadn't obeyed, God could've used another;

however, God WANTED to use Ananias. Just like God WANTED to use Saul/Paul. Sometimes you (being an Ananias, or a Saul) just have to release *it*.

What is God trying to release you from that you keep holding on to? Is it the old you? Is it the old way of thinking? Is it an old relationship? Maybe even old memories? What about feelings of anger/resentment for a wrong done to you in the past?

NEWSFLASH: You can't embrace the future (that stands before you) if you're holding on to the past (that lies behind you). You have to let go of your past so that you can hold on to your future. There is no way you'll be able to have them coexist together -- and to be frank, you should not even want them to. Your past might have been a perfect mixture of bad days and bright days, but your future has much better days. All perfect days? Of course not! Will you get hurt again? More than likely. But at least it's new, at least you are stronger than you were before, and at least you are not holding onto something that is old. That's the beauty of the future and so many of us miss out on it because we've allowed ourselves to live life filtered through a past that has expired so long ago.

Do yourself a favor: release every grudge that you may have. Holding grudges only hurts YOU...not the person you have the grudge against. I'm not saying that they didn't hurt you, I'm just saying let God heal you (how He sees fit to do so). Ananias had information that could have made him reject Saul, but he also had an understanding that it was possible for Saul to defy his perception by being different - so, he created space for that to happen by letting what COULD happen be greater than what had already happened in the past.

There is a very clear lesson in this story. Don't bind people to what they did because God can change them, too.

God can pull good out of anyone -- even the person who is most known for the bad they've done. Nobody is exempt from a touch of grace. God is SO great in power that He can convert those who had plans on killing you, and cause them to be a blessing to you instead! An one-track mindset can block that from happening, though. When your mind only understands, believes, and expects one thing from something or someone, nothing that is opposite of that mindset will happen. On the other hand, if you dare to believe that something beautiful can emerge from a place that has only produced pain, you'll experience something refreshingly amazing.

TODAY, be.Released from past hurts, frustrations, failures, and opinions of others - and be released into a new beginning.

On this eighth day, of this journey to a Royal Makeover, *be.Open* to A NEW BEGINNING... A FRESH START!

DAY NINE

"Who Loves U?"
Today's Scripture: 1 Corinthians 13 (Focus: v.1-8)

Love is a widespread subject. Almost everyone discusses it, loves it, gives it, and expects to receive it from the places it matters the most. While this is all very true, when the question "who loves you?" is asked, the answers vary and many of them prove that some don't know who loves them, some do not love themselves, some don't love God, and many have an inaccurate definition of what love actually is. And others, well, they are hanging somewhere in the balances of each scenario.

Do you know what your truth is concerning love? How would you answer if asked "who loves you?".

In these scriptures we are shown that your very best means nothing if it's not done in love. Your quest to be great, and do great things measures up to "a hill of beans" if you don't have love. This love requires you to love God, love your neighbor(s), love your enemies, AND love yourself. That is the whole focus of today's entry-- LOVING YOURSELF! It sounds so simple but it's the greatest battle most of us fight daily. For some of us, we are trying to find a reason to believe that we deserve to be loved by ourselves; and since we can't seem to find a reason, we look to find that love from other places and in the end, that void is still there waiting to be filled with the love that was meant to fit there.

The person that fails to love themselves seeks for substitutes to do it for them. Substitutes may get the job done but only for a limited amount of time. As a substitute teacher, I visit a lot of classrooms to fill in for absent teachers. In most cases, I do everything the original teacher would do if they were there but no matter how great I am at completing my duties for the day, regardless of how attached I become to the students, that assignment has an end date because I am only a substitute. It's the same way for some of you. In the classroom of Self-Love, you have let many substitutes fill in for you and at the end of the day, their assignment ends and the seat becomes empty in anticipation for the original teacher. How long will you wait for someone to love you in the way that you already have the capacity to love yourself?

What type of love are you focusing on?

Do you feel as if everyone, except you, is finding love?

Instead of focusing on being alone, find the joy in spending time with YOU! Learn how to embrace your own company. Use your alone time to explore the mysteries hidden in your greatness. There is so much about yourself that you have yet to discover. Instead of pretending to be someone you're not in order to gain the acceptance of a "crush", accept the God-given GRACE to be.U! By just being who you really are, you attract people who desire to be in your space because they see you and not a facade. Instead of searching for "love", be content with the love that you already have! In your heart, at this very moment, are unexplored dimensions of an amazing love waiting to touch you. Let it!

The love you think you haven't found yet ACTUALLY found you first! It's just waiting for you to find it. The good news? It doesn't require that you look far, you only need to look within to find it. When you finally find it, nothing about your life can stay the same. Not only will you begin to love yourself, but you'd be able to REALLY love God. Believe it or not, you can't really love Him (God) until you first know how to love you. How is this true? Just think about how, no matter what you do -- no matter how much you pray -- no matter how much you worship, there seems to still be a hunger that is unsatisfied. That is because your lack of love for yourself is impeding your ability to fully love God and receive His love in return. If you want to know how to love yourself, study the way that God loves you.

Your love life has just changed, and so did your confession. So, who loves you? YOU love you!

In your notes, write down the ways that you KNOW that God loves you --- His patience, His grace, His countless blessings on a daily basis. Then, list the ways that you can improve loving yourself or begin loving yourself. As always, be honest in your notes and pray for God to give you ways to daily love the way that HE does.

DAY TEN

"Will U Go Back(wards)?"
Today's Scripture: Exodus 14 (Focus: v.14-16)

In this passage of scripture Moses is leading the people of Israel out of slavery and bondage, and the Egyptians are following them. They get to what looks like an END and everyone is about to have a fit. God asked Moses the question, "Why do you cry to me? Tell the children of Israel to go forward." And those are the same instructions He's giving to you... GO FORWARD.

Have you been released from a place of bondage (physically, mentally, emotionally, spiritually)?
Were you set free and , as you were on your way out, the thing that released you pursued you once again?
This may be a very scary time for you; however, there is a decision to be made.

Will you be full of FAITH, or full of FEAR? Will you press onward in the direction of freedom? Or will you retreat and go BACK into bondage again? Will you fall back into a life that has NOTHING good for you all because you are too afraid to move forward? Don't go back(wards) because what stands before you seems too hard to conquer, and being a slave to your past seems "easier" and more "comfortable".

Following the path that leads forward can be terrifying when it seems as though you are marching toward defeat instead of victory. This is what happened to the clan of Israelites. The idea of moving forward did not scare them, the sight of what was in the distance did. They saw their enemies making their way to them and they were petrified because, in their mind, there was no way they could stand against this army. But God tells Moses to tell them to move on anyway and to use his staff to make a way for them to go through. You see what just happened here? They were essentially stressing over a problem they already had the solution to. So many of us do the same thing. We spend too much time crying about things God has given us the ability to handle on our own.

Remember one thing: If God sends you on the journey, it is already established in His will that you will arrive at the destination. Yes, you will encounter some unforeseen hassles. Yes, you will look into the distance and see some things you have no clue how you will handle -- but continue in a forward direction nonetheless. When that becomes hard to do, allow your mind to think on the words that Moses spoke to the Israelites: "Do not be afraid. Stand firm and you will see the deliverance the LORD will bring you today."

In your notes write down what hard place you may currently be standing in. List how you think going back would be beneficial to your process and to your personal growth. Once you've done that, list how your efforts of pressing onward (even through the hard places) will bring you out of bondage (physical, mental, spiritual, and emotional) and into your place of promise.

Anytime you get deep into your journey of moving on and you look ahead and it seems unfavorable, you are likely to think to yourself that maybe you should have stayed where you were to begin with, but that's not so. When you remain in a place God has given you permission to leave, you give yourself away to be a slave to your past. Make up your mind that this will NOT be the case for you! Trust that BETTER DAYS are AHEAD of you! The situation you're facing will NOT drown you. Trust God to be God. He'll cause you to walk across on dry ground! What stands before you...what you're about to walk into, though big and scary, is better than what you just walked out of! He will part your sea, but the choice to walk through is up to you!

DAY ELEVEN

"What Do U Have to Give?"
Today's Scripture: John 6 (Focus: V. 9-12)
Matthew 25 (Focus: v. 15-28)

Sacrifice. What is sacrifice? And how does sacrifice affect you? In one of today's passage of scripture a little boy sacrificed his meal as an offering, and because of his sacrifice thousands were fed. In the other passage of scripture a man sacrificed his increase because of fear and intimidation. In both passages, what each individual had could have been viewed as a small portion; however, the difference in the outcome is noted in how the portion was handled.

Do you find yourself constantly comparing yourself (gifts, talents, abilities) to those around you? Do you constantly fight with the thought or feelings of everyone being better, smarter, and more capable than you---offering so much more than you?

Well, *PUMP YOUR BRAKES*!

It's time to stop taking inventory of what everyone else is bringing to the table and focus on what you have to give, and what you bring to the table. You are not the same as everyone else; you're different, so you cannot expect your sacrifice to look like the next person's. You have a sacrifice that no one else can offer to God.

God has gifted you; will you give Him a return on His investment? Will you work the gift(s) and talent(s) He's given you to increase the Kingdom, to expand your church, to enrich your community, and impact the lives of all you encounter? Or will you, instead, give Him your complaints? Will you tell Him how He gave your other two friends five and two talents, but only gave you ONE (so you buried it)?

This thing belongs to you but what if you chose to SHARE it? How many could it bless? What if you chose to WORK it? What increase would it yield? Your dance, your song, your "hand" -- how many lives would be touched, changed even, just because you sacrificed for the greater good! Never think that what you have is not enough. "Little" is never really "a little" when you place it in God's hands. In God's hands, that which appears to not be much is ALWAYS "all you need". If you focus too much on the surface of your gifts and talents, you will sacrifice with a speculation that they are not enough for God or others.

He gave it to you, can you give it back?

So, today, make the choice to work YOUR gift. In order to activate your gifts, you have to acknowledge what they are. In your notes, name them one by one and list ways that you can sacrifice them to be of service in an amazing way. And maybe you have already identified what your gifts are, but you have been a bit stagnant lately because you feel like there isn't more. There is always more. There are always ways to improve and maximize your gifts, but you may have to search for opportunities to expand and sharpen them. God will even connect us to mentors, employers, Pastors, who will at times see gifts that we've yet to recognize and not only help reveal them to us, but also cultivate and pull them out of us.

If you're unsure of what your gift is, then ask Him to reveal it to you. He's your maker, He KNOWS what He placed inside of you! It's important to note that the gifts are already placed inside of you. This means that they are already prepared and you do not have to search outside of yourself or God to locate your gift. The treasure that is your gift has been wrapped in your earthen vessel. Look for it there. God strategically placed your gift in you to avoid you looking outside of His will for what's already in you.

DAY TWELVE

"What Did He Send U To Do?"
Today's Scripture: Judges 6 (Focus: v.12-16)

In this passage of scripture we see Gideon, who is intimidated by those he views to be greater than he is, threshing wheat in the wine-press in order to hide from them. Gideon was small in his own eyes and saw his situation through fearful eyes. While he was hiding, an Angel of the Lord appeared to him and spoke to him. However, he didn't speak to the little boy "Gideon", he spoke to "Gideon, the mighty man of valor". At the time Gideon was actually being a "punk" (for lack of a better term) but The Lord, KNOWING Gideon, spoke to who he REALLY was.

Many people see you as small because that's how you see yourself. When you decide to see yourself as small, you will think everyone else to be superior. How you feel about yourself is easily seen by others, but the great thing is that God knows who you really are even when you do not. And THAT is who He speaks to when He speaks to you! It's not that He does not see the false view that you hold in your mind of yourself; He just disregards it because His words are meant for the authentic version of who you are. If God lent His words to nurture our falsehoods, greatness in the Earth would be foreign.

Gideon was so shocked by what he was being told that he would accomplish that he asked for several forms of proof. Does this sound familiar? It might remind you of yourself because similar to Gideon, you need proof before you move on to producing what God has given you to do. The moment you see that what is being asked of you falls out of alignment with your limited idea of yourself, you deem it unreal and require additional information to legitimize your assignment and your qualifications to carry it out. This is exactly what Gideon did. He couldn't see how he could have been chosen for such a task. Others couldn't see it, he couldn't see it, but God did. You see, who you REALLY are may very well contradict everything everyone else has told you that you are, possibly everything that they think you are, and maybe everything that YOU think that you are. That is why it is so imperative that you find out who God says that you are! And after you find out what God says concerning you, begin to believe it and move in the direction that leads to a destiny that reflects God's thoughts and plans of you. When you do this, you will always live life at YOUR greatest level, in a lane that was carved specifically for you.

Have you always pictured yourself as "normal"? Have you only aspired to do normal things in life, but for some reason your normal things NEVER work out the way you planned them to? Or maybe "normal" has produced some kind of success for you, but after the height of it fades, you feel dissatisfied because somewhere in the corridors of your soul, you know that there is more for you to do?

Well, maybe that's because you're being called from a place of "normalcy" and sent to a place of GREATNESS! In the realm of greatness, limits and barriers do not exist unless you create them yourself.

You are shocked by the weight of the assignment given to you because you don't yet see who He sees every time He looks upon you. The mere fact that you were chosen for the assignment is proof that you have the grace and potential to not only do it, but to do it exceptionally well. Today, see yourself through His eyes, and trust that He'll be with you as you go do what He sent you to do! The eyes of the Lord searched the Earth, and when He could have sent anyone else, He intentionally decided to send you. Why? It's because He knows that you have what it takes, and you have something that someone else needs. You never know who is waiting for you to arrive (mentally, physically, spiritually) so that they can be released to be who they are [family, friends, neighbors, etc.].

be.Open (EPATHA) to a NEW YOU, a NEW ASSIGNMENT, and a NEW DIRECTION! In your notes, write down the thing(s) that you feel about those three NEW things, and then write down all you've been hearing God say to you about them.

"Go in this might of yours... Have I not sent you?"
Judges 6:14

DAY THIRTEEN

"Are U Loyal?"
Today's Scripture: Ruth 1 (Focus: v.13-18)

In this passage of scripture we see Naomi's daughter-in-law, Ruth, and they have both suffered great heartbreak in the loss of Naomi's son/Ruth's husband. Ruth could have easily made the choice to return to her home, return to the god of her family, and simply wave goodbye to Naomi and everything attached to her. But she didn't. Loyalty made her stay when leaving was an easy option.

I have experienced loss and set-back, and I have, at times, contemplated returning to where I came from. Going back to my family's home seemed to be the best choice for me. It seemed like a "quick fix" to my circumstances and my annoying, draining, uncomfortable situations. There were many points when I became very frustrated with my process and felt as if I needed an "OUT"! It didn't matter that it would get better eventually; it didn't matter that it would work together for my good. None of that mattered. When the situation was in no way favorable to me, I wanted out because remaining loyal to my process came with pain I couldn't endure anymore.

NUGGET: Don't abort your promise trying to avoid the pain that comes with the "process". If you can just get through the pain of the process, the promise that you'll bring forth will all be worth it!

Ruth, no doubt, endured pain but she was loyal to her commitment and her assignment. In life we are faced with choices. You can choose to be comfortable, or you can choose to be loyal; and NO, sometimes you can't do both. In fact, there's no real way to do both. Loyalty doesn't offer much comfort; it always has an intense level of discomfort. Considering that, it's no mystery why being loyal is such a struggle these days. If being loyal was easy, it would be more common. But because it's not, many people decide to go with what is convenient --- *comfort.*

Have you been proven loyal? Yes? Have you made sure that your loyalties are to the right THINGS and to the right ONE(s)?

Sometimes loyalty to your assignment and purpose...loyalty to your destiny...may cause you to have to separate from some of the things and people that you know and love. When it does, instead of fighting, learn to be okay with it. Separation can be hurtful but in the grand scheme of things, it saves you a lot of wasted time and heartache. It's a lot better to feel the temporary sting of separation than endure the brutal blow of *no good* connections. The connections that have run their course cloud your vision and cripple your ability to nurture your assignment and your purpose because you are exerting energy into something useless; also known as casting your pearls before swine.

On this journey, you have to be disciplined enough to not maintain loyalty to anything or anyone that does not benefit who you are, where you are headed, and what you have been trusted to do in the earth. For Ruth, her loyalty kept her from going backwards and it helped her stay connected with the person and path meant for HER journey. When you get a firm grip on loyalty with a clear understanding of what your life is meant for, you make informed decisions and wiser investments of your loyalty.

Choose to remain faithful to where God is taking you. Remain loyal to every part of your process, and the timing of your process, so that you can enjoy the rewards of your promise! In the absence of due process, there is no space for promised blessings. I know that, sometimes we want everything without going through anything, but it will never work that way.

In your notes, write down those things that you have

been loyal/faithful to, and determine if those things are in line with your purpose. No wasted time on things and people who are not purposed to go where God is leading you!

No dead weight!

Push forward!

Destiny is waiting!

DAY FOURTEEN

"Will U Work For It?"
Today's Scripture: Genesis 29 (Focus: v. 9-11; 18-30)

In this passage we see Jacob who has met Rachel at the well and, stunned by her beauty, he has fallen for her. Jacob wanted Rachel, and told her father that he would work for him for seven years in order to have Rachel's hand in marriage. He worked all seven of those years seemingly without complaint because he loved Rachel so much. Verse 20 of Genesis 29 says it like this: "So Jacob served seven years for Rachel, and they seemed only a few days to him because of the love he had for her".

Very easily, Jacob shows us what it means to "want it bad enough". He didn't stop at just wanting Rachel as a wife, he found a plan to make marrying her a reality. The lesson in this is rather simple, and that is: you don't want it bad enough until you're willing to work for it no matter the time it will take to get it. Are you looking for real results? If so, there has to be a marriage between your "want" and your "work". Unless the two are harmoniously fit together, you'll be stuck with a lot of passion, but no tangible evidence of your passion.

When it came time to seal the deal, Laban, Rachel's father, tricked Jacob by giving him Leah to marry instead of Rachel. Can you imagine this happening to you? Who works seven years at one goal just to have deception be their reward? To have a lie presented to you after you've given time, sweat, and tears to something is a brutal blow to your faith. It's one thing if you failed to honestly work for something, but it's a different ballgame when you're cheated unfairly.

It goes without saying that this had to trouble Jacob's spirit and put him on the edge. Yet, he wouldn't let this be his end. Not giving up hope, Jacob knew what and who he wanted and REFUSED to settle. He settled in his mind that it was worth another try. In order to get Rachel's hand, he agreed to work another seven years for Laban. In persisting, Jacob teaches us all a powerful life lesson: refuse to trade your truth for a lie.

What really inspired Jacob's persistence even after being tricked? Was it deeper than Rachel's beauty and the physical attraction that he had for her? It had to be. If it were not, my opinion is that he would have washed his hands of the entire pursuit when Laban deceived him, yet he didn't. He stayed. He remained passionate. He was determined to not take a replacement for his promise. But why? I choose to believe it was because in his spirit, He knew Rachel was written on the pages of Heaven's perfect will for his life. When your spirit knows what Heaven has willed for you, your desire becomes to live that out on earth.

Is there something that you really want--something that you've had your heart set on for years? Do you think of, or dream of, it often? Do you have the faith to believe that it can one day, possibly even one day SOON, be yours?

If you answered "YES" to all of the above questions, I have one more question for you: WILL YOU WORK FOR IT? This question is what makes the difference between living a dream and just having a dream.

You can dream dreams all night and day, but will you WAKE UP and actually begin to work on making those dreams a reality? If God has placed a desire in your heart, if He has made you passionate about something, don't stop working until you see it come to fruition. The moment that you become serious about your passions, purpose, desires, and dreams---you will stop at nothing to make them happen. Not time, inconvenience, fear, or anything else can separate you from your dream when you really want it

The process begins with identifying what you want and then making the strides necessary for the desired results. We often hear it said, and I'm sure many of us say it ourselves, that one should trust their process. And I wholeheartedly agree. Trusting your process is important; but trusting the timing of your process is crucial. Without faith in the timing of the journey that you're on, you'll find yourself agitated and discouraged because things are either happening too quickly or too slow for you.

Trust every second of your process and be okay with the speed God moves it at. Whether frightfully slow or extremely fast, trust it. Jacob explained that 7 years only seemed like a few days to him. To me, that insinuates two things. First, his passion to win Rachel for a wife overshadowed the movement of time. Secondly, I believe that Jacob learned how to trust and enjoy the timing of the process.

In your notes, write down what it is that you want, what God has made you truly passionate about, and THEN pray for a strategy. The purpose of having a strategy is to build a plan to make your goals tangible. Once your strategy is revealed, write it down, and honestly evaluate it and answer the question: am I truly willing to work for this? Before you answer, consider every possibility that can unfold during your pursuit.

If your answer is yes:

PURSUE

PERSIST

WIN

DAY FIFTEEN

"Do U Need a Refill?"
Today's Scripture: John 4 (Focus v.15)

In this passage of scripture Jesus met with the woman at the well, and although He knew all of her indiscretions, and all of her "secrets", He still offered her a better life. That's what He seeks to do for you while on this journey. The whole purpose for these 30 days is to be made new by Jesus. At different points, the quest to a better life can leave you feeling empty, feeling like you are running on nothing but faith and fumes. That's okay, because in a strange way, that likely means that you're closer to being better. More importantly, the saving grace is, you don't have to remain drained. God is always prepared to give you a refill if you'll pause long enough to receive it. The well didn't lose water, we just stopped showing up to draw from it.

Most long trips traveled in a car begin on a full tank of gas. The further the car goes, the more gas the car exhausts. Therefore, at some point, the driver has to pull over in order to refuel their tank so they can arrive at their expected destination. It is not much different on this spiritual journey you're traveling on. The energy, faith, and hope that you started with has to be renewed at some point or you will crash and burn. It's not fair to yourself to lose a chance at getting to the finish line because you didn't know when to slow down and pour back into your endurance tank.

In the focus scripture for today, the Samaritan woman that met Jesus at the well says something very key. She tells Jesus to give her the water so that she doesn't have to keep coming there to draw water. In other words, she was tired of settling for temporary satisfaction, and she was finally ready for something that could fill her. Now, does this mean that after Jesus filled her that time she would no longer need to be filled ever again? Of course not. There will be many moments of refilling, but the refill has to come from the right source. The bottom line is: ONLY JESUS CAN FILL YOUR SOUL. In His presence, that's where you'll find times of refreshing and refill. It matters not what area of your life needs a refill, it just matters that you know where to go to be filled again.

Today, be filled again. Let Him "give you living water"! It can be as simple as lifting up your cup. It doesn't have to be really "DEEP", or even really hard. A simple petition saying "God, fill me up" can unlock exactly what you need from God for the remainder of your journey.

Do you feel drained? Do you feel as if you don't have enough "juice" left for the journey?

Well, that isn't surprising. You are half-way through your journey, and I'm sure it is (or has been at some point or another) extremely overwhelming for you. Even with that in mind, this is DEFINITELY not the point where you give in, or up. At this point in your journey, you only need to be refilled. It doesn't have to end because you're empty, unless you allow it to. The solution to conquering emptiness is getting a refill, not quitting.

Have a clear understanding of what your emptiness means. Why are you empty? What do you need from God to fill that void? Are you trying to fill a place God intentionally left empty? If you misinterpret your emptiness, you can make the mistake of using the wrong things to get a refill, or even worse, you will quit instead of being quenched. On a spiritual journey such as this one, distraction is the enemy's favorite tactic to derail you. He wants nothing more than for you to make one wrong decision that will throw you completely off course. But as long as you know that Jesus is the ultimate source for you, you won't trust anything else to fill you , or allow anything to remove your feet from your set path.

This will be the making of a great week, complete with a new level of refreshing, and deeper/more meaningful insight! You're getting BETTER!

In your notes, write down the areas of your life that you need/want to be filled in. Before you ask God to fill those areas, make sure your requests match His will for your journey, and ultimately, your life.

DAY SIXTEEN

"Who Will U Call?"
Today's Scripture: Jeremiah 29 (Focus: v.12-14)

In this passage of scripture, Jeremiah wrote a letter to the captives taken away by Nebuchadnezzar from Jerusalem to Babylon. And the word of the Lord came in this letter reassuring them that even though they were taken captive, the Lord had a plan for their lives. He told them that He knew the plans He had for them--that they would call on Him and He would listen; that they would seek Him and find Him when they searched for Him with all their heart, and that He would bring them back from captivity. In essence, God was saying to them that regardless of their circumstances, there was still a plan for their lives that far exceeded all they were experiencing. God wanted them to understand that despite being in captivity, their bondage didn't revoke the access they had to His presence.

When your problem(s) hold you captive it is great to have friends around you, in your corner, standing beside you, in an attempt to pull you out of whatever you're in, BUT when things TRULY "hit the fan" who will you call? When life has seemingly stripped you of the hope that you had hidden in your heart, what is your next move? If the questions you need answered can't be answered by human connections, where do you turn?

Will you call on those who will take in the information of your captivity, but can do nothing to free you? Will you call on the one who is holding you captive, and beg them to release you? Or will you call on The One who can break every chain of bondage and captivity?

Sometimes when we're in a rut, we attempt to call on others, but they can't/don't come through for us how we expect them to. Either they do nothing at all or they do the bare minimum. And to be honest, I don't necessarily believe that happens just because our friends and family members are "flaky". I believe, that in some instances, we're rejected so that we can seek God instead of people. A lot of times, God will allow people to disappoint you just so you can learn to depend on Him. After enough disappointment, you eventually learn to make God your first stop instead of your last resort.

It would do you so much better to go directly to God and seek Him for direction; and let everything else happen the way that it's meant to. You know the most amazing thing about seeking God? It's already promised that if you seek Him with your whole heart, you will find Him. God is always waiting for us; all we need to do is show up where He is.

So often we have the RIGHT conversation, but it's with the WRONG people. I'm not saying not to ever share your problems with those close to you, but I am saying to make a conscious decision to seek The One who has the answers to it ALL. We are all of the same body, joined together by the same God, so it's really okay to enjoy the benefits of a faith-based community, but you have to learn how to maintain God as your primary contact person. It should never be your truth that you call on people more than you call on God.

In your notes, write down all of the "problems" you have and write down the person(s) you've told about your problem. Also, write down how they've helped you (if at all), and look to see if you've subconsciously depended on that person/those people more than God. Lastly, figure out a way to trust God MORE, and earnestly work on it.

DAY SEVENTEEN

"Are U Disciplined?"
Today's Scripture: Isaiah 58 (Focus v. 6)

Many times as a child I, like many others, couldn't wait to make it to "adulthood" because I thought that equaled "FREEDOM FROM RULES, REGULATIONS, and DISCIPLINE". But what I, like many others, found out once I actually hit adulthood is that I need the same amount (if not more) of each of those things – RULES, REGULATIONS, and DISCIPLINE – to live a balanced and productive life. If you're reading this and you have made your transition into adulthood, I bet you agree with me on this.

The focus scripture talks about a fast that has been chosen and generated specifically for you and the purpose that it serves. What is a fast? A fast is defined as a period of abstaining or self-denial from something, specifically the things that take up most of our time and attention -- be it a daily activity, food items, or favorite television show. A fast is a period of selfless sacrifice that demands strong discipline.

It is important to note that a fast is not a gimmick for the purpose of shedding the extra pounds gained from overindulgence of your favorite foods and snacks. Neither is fasting only about refraining from certain activities and such; it goes much deeper than that. Fasting, as described in the focus scripture, is designed "to loose the bonds of wickedness, to undo the heavy burdens, to let the oppressed go free, and to break every yoke..." You see, true fasting is about self-restraint, being disciplined, and following rules and regulations in order to manifest supernatural results such as those aforementioned. When all your period of fasting brings about is a loss in weight, you have been dieting. When your time of fasting brings about immeasurable change on a spiritual level, you've done it the right way.

Fasting-- an activity that must have discipline at its core -- teaches us the hard lesson of denying ourselves and ignoring our personal desires that would make us miss out on what is good for us and our life, and ultimately pleasing to God. Think about fasting the same way that one would perceive dieting. Dieting, although it incorporates discipline, the yielded results are more than just slimming down. Whenever you diet and do it appropriately, you're healthier, stronger, and in a better state of well-being. Likewise, proper fasting brings on endless benefits that increase you spiritually, and brings forth a more grounded and unique version of YOU.

Are you someone that always does whatever you want to do, whenever you want to do it, just because you can? If yes, how is that working out for you?

Today, I encourage you to implement some form of discipline into your life. The decision to be disciplined is one that you have to make daily. A new day needs a new measure of commitment to being disciplined. Every morning that you awake to start your day, it is your responsibility to focus on doing whatever it takes to be grounded. The more consistency you give to discipline, the more power you give it to transform into a lifestyle. And that is what discipline was designed to be, a lifestyle. It is a lifestyle that you must commit to, and it's applicable to every area of your life (spiritual, mental, emotional, as well as physical).

What feels good to you may not always be good for you, and vice versa. What doesn't feel good TO you, may actually be good FOR you in the long run. So, maybe there are some things that you like that you can no longer indulge in. Perhaps there are foods that you love--that are unhealthy for you; people that you like being around--that are toxic for you; places that you enjoy going to--that may cause your character to be questioned.

Learn to tell yourself "NO" to some things sometimes. Authentic discipline is the ability to acknowledge that just because you *can* do something, it doesn't mean that you *should* do it. Discipline is not synonymous with perfection. Quite frankly, when you give yourself to striving for discipline, you realize that aiming for perfection is both unreal and unnecessary. As long as you're able to have and maintain self-control, you will never have to frustrate yourself with the unrealistic goal of being perfect.

In your notes, write down the forms of discipline that work best for you. List the ones that will cause you to feel better, live better, and *BE BETTER!*

DAY EIGHTEEN

"Did They Drop U? Or did they...?"
Today's Scripture: 2 Samuel 4 (Focus: v. 4)
2 Samuel 9 (Focus: v. 7-11)

Mephibosheth, as a 5 year old child, was dropped by the one who was supposed to take care of him, the one who was in charge of protecting him. As a result of his "caretaker's" negligence, although unintentional, he became lame and stuck in "Lo Debar". Lo Debar wasn't his inheritance; he was there because of an accident that inconvenienced him. It didn't matter what got him there though, the truth about his life was that he was royalty and he didn't belong where his caretaker's mistake left him.

Have you ever been dropped before? Maybe the drop you suffered was figurative and not literal such as the one that Mephibosheth endured. Figurative falls do, however, have the same impact as literal falls, because they inflict damage of some sort. No matter if it is physically, mentally, spiritually, or emotionally, a fall will damage you in some kind of way. Not only will a fall damage you, it will land you in a space that was never meant to be inhabited by you. But you don't have to stay there. The only time a place of pain becomes permanent is when you allow yourself to become content and you don't desire to live outside of the place where you were dropped.

Soooo, who dropped you? The answer to this question may be derived from the way that you perceive things or it could be derived from the way things actually occurred. Either way, it is NOW up to you to make the decision to move forward from it. HOW you move forward will be determined by how you choose to see your situation. If you feel DROPPED, you may have to 'get up' before you can move forward... but by ALL MEANS, PLEASE get up and move forward.

Every drop is not an act of betrayal although some are. Still, betrayal or not, what if you made the choice to see it as them "releasing you" instead? Has a different "feel". doesn't it? That is because this scenario is advantageous. Why? It is better to be released rather than held onto when the connection is no longer beneficial. Being released will conflict with your emotions, as it should, but think about the long term suffering holding on could cause. Our emotions are flustered by certain releases from some people because at some point we convinced ourselves that life wouldn't be possible without them. Then, to our surprise, God introduces us to our own strength and we see that all we truly need is His presence.

Even in seeing things from this perspective, realize that you may have to stand still for a moment before taking the first step (because honestly, walking on your own for the first time may cause a little apprehension). The bottom line is, forward movement is a MUST. It doesn't matter how big your first step forward is as long as you make one. A small step forward is still a step toward progression. And that's what it's always about--forward movement. Sure, you're going to have to figure out your own way, but God promises to order every one of your steps. So you might be scared but you'll never have to walk alone and you'll always be heading in a forward direction, moving away from the place where you were dropped.

When you keep the point of view that "they dropped me", you feel entitled to place and use it as an excuse. On the other side of it, when you think "they just released me", you want to know what better thing you're being released into, and then, you conjure up the faith to explore what is on the other side of what you have been released from. A release is an introduction to something new and something better. A release may be unplanned and unexpected but in the end, it all works together to produce something good.

You will never walk into what God has for you if you're still stuck in what you were actually supposed to go through! Don't miss what's happening for you now because you can't let go of what happened to you back then. Yes, you were dropped and yes, it did hurt and it might have even changed your mental/emotional condition; but it did not alter the purpose for your creation. The purpose you were created for will exist during and after your pain. I pray that you would understand that being "lame" doesn't change who you really are, and I pray you will realize that you can never live the moments God has planned for you by holding onto what hurt you.

In your notes, write down any issue(s) that you feel has "handicapped" you, and when you've gotten it down, write down how you're going to move forward in spite of those issues. Moving on is not impossible but you need a solid plan of action to accomplish doing so. God can use you, even with your issues, but be reminded that He can and He wants to heal you of them as well. Open your heart wide enough for healing to be poured on your broken pieces.

DAY NINETEEN

"Will U Be the One?"
Today's Scripture: Ezekiel 22 (Focus v. 30)

No matter how old or how young you are, you can see the things that happen in the world we live in, and know that it (and us) are in DESPERATE need of prayer. In this passage of scripture, the land was full of corruption, and the Lord was looking for a man to intercede on behalf of the land so that He wouldn't have to destroy it. Unfortunately, He sought for just one person, but He found no one. I wonder what the reason was for there not being at least one person available who could find the time to pray on behalf of the land. Could it have been that everyone was busy with their daily duties so they were spiritually disconnected from the world around them? Or perhaps it could have been that their main focus was everything that was corrupt and falling to pieces in their own lives? Many of us find it difficult to get into a posture of prayer when life has become an unbearable burden for us. Rather than being the one to pray, we prefer someone to pray for us.

Not only do we feel that the world in which we live is in turmoil, we sometimes feel that way about our personal lives. We go through situations in life that are uncomfortable, and we often wonder "why?" We ask ourselves what did we do to deserve certain plights without realizing that God only allowed us to be tried because He trusts the strength that He placed inside of us to endure and conquer. Furthermore, although it is not always in the way we prefer, He has every intention to deliver us from every trial we encounter in life.

Whenever life has your back to the wall and you feel like there is no possible way that you can keep going, remember that because you love the Lord, and you have been called according to His purpose, everything HAS to work together for your good. That isn't a possibility, it's a promise. The world around you may seem bleak and void of hope, but your God is watching over every word He has spoken about you, and He's waiting to perform them. God is not only waiting to give you a miracle; but He is preparing you to BE a miracle in the Earth for someone else. It is for this reason that He is looking for someone to get in the gap.

Today's pain is tomorrow's purpose. Later, down the road, you will realize that you experienced those things in order to be able to help a brother/sister in the same predicament. Storms create our stories; our stories become tools of hope in the Earth for someone that has lost their way. The amazing thing about a story of triumph is that it evolves into a seed of intercession. Have you ever heard of someone dealing with something that you survived and your first response to it is prayer? If that's the case with you, that means that your story is not just a testimony but it's momentum that pushes you into the gap to pray.

Your prayers can be the anchor that rescues someone from drifting. In the gap, we are given the chance to be selfless and compassionate. In the gap, that's where we forget about ourselves and esteem someone above our personal needs and priorities. When we're in the gap, we prevent God from coming up empty handed when He surveys the land looking for an intercessor.

Will you take a day out of your "personal journey" to stand in the gap for someone else?

Will you be the one?

Will you intercede?

When you stand in the gap for someone else, what you're praying for God to do for them, by way of ORDER, hits you first! He cares for you, too! God will never expect you to labor in prayer and not reward your sacrifice. He seeks to provide you everything that you have petitioned Him for.

In your notes, write down those things/situations/pitfalls in your life that you know you were able to walk over/across/through because the prayers of an intercessor built a bridge for you. Recall when the prayers of an intercessor filled in those gaps for you. Now, think about people you know who may be going through similar situations, and commit to standing in the gap for them, too! Can't think of anyone who is battling something you conquered? Well, commit to praying for someone who is going through SOMETHING. It doesn't have to be a close friend or relative -- your prayers reach people and places that you can't. Send a prayer to Heaven on someone's behalf today.

DAY TWENTY

"Are U Prepared For It?"
Today's Scripture: 1 Samuel 17 (Focus v.40-51)

The giant, Goliath, is up ready for battle and he's telling the armies of Israel to choose someone to join in the battle against him. The armies of Israel have sized this giant up and everyone, including Saul, is afraid. Oh, but not David! David was the youngest son of Jesse and while three of his older brothers followed Saul, he stayed behind to tend his father's sheep. Many discounted David's job as a shepherd, but they didn't even know that was his training ground. David told Saul, "Let no man's heart fail because of him; your servant will go and fight with this Philistine." (v. 32). Saul, looking at David's size and stature, put his equipment on him, but that was no good for David. David knew his strengths, but more than that, he knew and trusted in God's strength.

People have "sized you up" and, merely looking at your outward appearance, have already judged what they think you're capable of doing and what you cannot do. They've tried putting their equipment on you, but it was not made for you! What people fail to realize is that God called you, trained you, equipped you, and PREPARED you long before you got to THIS battle. You didn't need their equipment, all you needed was the opportunity.

David said, "I cannot walk with these for I have not tested them". You know what works for YOU! You know what does not work for you. In this moment, David was inadvertently teaching them that it is not wise to fight with what has not been tested. The battle ahead of David was far too great to lose it by wearing equipment that was not tailored to fit him. Yes, it was made for fighting, and yes, there may have been some victories won by others who wore it. However, it was never worn or tested by David and, therefore, it was not suitable for the fight.

Take off everything that everyone else has tried to put on you that does not fit who you are, and what you have been called to do. Trying to wear what wasn't tailored to fit you will make you lose at things you were supposed to win at. Now, don't misinterpret my point. There is nothing wrong with being helped. In fact, I am a firm believer that God provides assistance for every assignment...but He never provides assistance that doesn't match your assignment. The surest way to identify whether or not the help someone is offering you is from God is by measuring the fit of their agenda. If their agenda needs any alterations or adjustments, that's not the help that God wants you to have. Help from God doesn't come with an agenda that needs to be adjusted because it shows up with a perfect fit.

What has God called you to do? Who is He training you to be? Is it to be an entrepreneur? Is it to be a CEO? Is it to be an author? What steps have you taken to own your own business? Is it to be at the top of your class? What have you done to increase your scholastic performance? Is it to be married? How have you prepared yourself to become a "wife"?

God calling and choosing you for a position does not negate the fact that it must be coupled with work done on your part. It is also perfectly fine to WANT things in this season of your life. But know that you must couple your "WANT" with "WORK". Getting to "that place" might require a fight, but you don't have to worry, just be prepared. As long as you're prepared, there's no way that you can lose. Proper preparation guarantees that you will succeed at what you're working towards. To be prepared really just means that you have a plan in place; it means that you have full understanding of what God has given you to do as well as what you want to do, and you've created a reasonable plan of action to accomplish it all.

Do you have a plan? If you do, have you been sticking to it consistently? If you don't have a plan, how are you expecting to be prepared for any part of what God wants to use your life for? You need a plan to get you from wanting and working to winning. As long as you're without a plan, you'll just be *wanting* without ever making any progress or strides towards what you want to win. With a plan, you're unstoppable and winning is inevitable. I've said it earlier on and I'll reinforce it here: GOD HONORS A PLAN! Every plan that you commit to God, He promises to prosper it. God cannot provide grace for a plan that does not exist.

On Day 4 of this journey, your task was to write down your vision so that you could get a sense of where you are going. Now, at Day 20, with only a few more days left of this Royal Makeover, I imagine that you have settled on where you are going, or you at least have a good idea by now. With that being the case, I have a question for you: when you get to the destination, will you be prepared for what's awaiting you there? As you can see, preparation is paramount. Knowing where you are going, writing the vision and having a plan to get there is for naught without adequate preparation.

In your notes, write down what God has called/chosen you to do, and then write down ways to prepare for it. As you continue the rest of this journey and even on the days after this journey has ended, remember this simple formula: **Want + Work = WIN!**

DAY TWENTY-ONE

"Will U Build It?"
Today's Scripture: Genesis 6 (Focus v.14-22)

In the "stormy" seasons of life it can sometimes feel as if you're out in the deep end, you can't swim, and you have NO BOAT. Imagine being in the middle of the water with the shore at a far distance and you have no idea how you are going to survive. Not a good feeling, is it? As life's storms start to rage, you often ask, "God, why so much rain? And why all at ONCE?" But did you ever stop to ask yourself THIS: "Did God ask me to do something that I said "no" to?" Maybe you were too consumed with doing what you WANTED to do. Or perhaps you just ignored it because "SURELY He couldn't have been talking to OR about YOU!! You have NO CLUE how to do what He's asking of you". Maybe, just MAYBE, you could sail through your stormy season a little better if you would just be obedient -- BUILD IT -- do what He's called you to do.

In this passage of scripture, God was grieved with man, and was going to destroy man; but ONE man, Noah, found grace in the eyes of God. One thing about God, He doesn't need a multitude; He only needs one willing vessel in order to accomplish major things in the Earth. Noah was that one willing vessel who found grace (favor) in God's sight. It's a beautiful thing to know that you have found favor with your God. To be honest, that should truly be one of our foremost and deepest passions as we go throughout each day. When you've won favor with God, He will trust you with major assignments and crown you with a special grace.

God graced Noah to do something that he had never done before. It was new. It was fresh. It was different. There was no manual with instructions outlining the "how to". There was no template to answer his questions or soothe any of the doubts running through his mind. But all he had to do was listen, follow the voice of God, and be obedient. God gave him every instruction he needed to accomplish the very thing He had graced him to do. Noah didn't need the facts, he only needed faith to begin what God was trusting him to achieve. It's the same with you. You don't need the facts, you only need faith to get started. Your faith will prompt God's voice and He will begin to speak everything that you need to hear to get the job done. As God speaks, listen and follow His lead. Of course, that's easy to say and hard to do, but be confident that it can be done. The bottom line of the matter is: our job is to START and FINISH; God's job is to handle everything in between.

Over these next nine days, discover and/or rediscover what God has called you to do. You know exactly what it is. That one thing that you wake up with on your heart; that one thing that you're so scared of yet so passionate about. It is that thing that is waiting for you to begin and complete it. The most hopeful part of it all? You don't have to do any of it alone. Everything that has been given to you to do by God comes with sufficient grace and guidance. Trust God, day-by-day, to provide you with the instructions, strategies, AND resources needed.

In your notes, write down everything that God is saying and revealing about what he has you working on.

What do you need to do? Who are you supposed to connect with to build? Are there any details that you should be giving close attention to?

You need to write everything down, no matter how insignificant you think it to be, write it anyway. There are people coming after you who will need it! God knows that this is bigger than you. Considering that, He is going to appoint someone somewhere to assist you who has exactly what you need. Be ready with a written plan when they arrive so that they can read the vision and run with it.

The GRACE is on you...get to building!

DAY TWENTY-TWO

"Face It! He Chose U?"
Today's Scripture: 2 Thessalonians 2 (Focus v. 13-17)

Sometimes when we think of our life's plan, and then look at the way our life is taking place, it's hard to understand it all. It can be hard to have hope in a plan that looks so opposite to your present reality. How do you really trust a plan that seems to be overshadowed by the trouble piling itself up on your plate? While your life may seem "surreal" at times, it is indeed your life nonetheless, so just FACE IT! (Smile.) Take a deep breath and accept that although you don't have the power to choose the course for your life, you were still chosen by God.

What does it mean to be chosen? To be chosen means that you were strategically selected with a particular purpose in mind. If you are chosen by a recruiting officer for a certain job that means you have something to offer that meets the requirements of the position that is looking to be filled. In the same way, when God was in need of someone that could handle everything your assignment in the earth would entail, He counted you as worthy and then He chose you. You weren't just placed on Earth, you were sent here to live out the reasons why you were chosen.

This passage confirms that He chose you -- The ALL-KNOWING, ALL-WISE GOD -- chose YOU!! No, it wasn't a "slip up", and it most certainly wasn't by accident that you ended up in your mother's womb or here on Earth. He purposefully chose you! The very instant that He blew breath into your body that was the same second He set you aside from the rest and handpicked you to blaze a peculiar trail that NO ONE else has the grace to travel. Sure, they may have a parallel or similar trail, but most definitely not your exact one. Do you comprehend how special you really are to God? The love of God runs so deep for you that He loves you too much to let you share lanes with the next person. Others might have a similar calling, they may even be called to do the same thing as you but in a different way and a different place, but absolutely no one can live in your lane.

What did He choose you for? I'm not sure....but God is. Your "what" is no mystery to the God that has masterfully authored every detail of your life -- including the ones you have yet to step into. Your sovereign God knows what He chose, created, and called you for. You should ask Him for the details. Ask Him to unveil the plans that He has for you. Might they be heavy? Perhaps. Will it be a lot of responsibility? Probably so! But you are equipped for it!

Do you really want what He has in store for you?

Will you follow through in doing

what He's chosen you to do?

Everything you have walked through in these past 3 weeks (21 days) has helped you to come a little closer with this purpose… with destiny… YOUR DESTINY! Don't get so caught up in the "I can't believe He chose me" that you make it hard for Him to actually USE you! Accept that God chose you and then allow God to use you! Since we're on the topic of being used by God, allow me to caution you to never be prideful about what He's chosen you to do! He doesn't NEED you, but He chooses to INCLUDE you! Whether you know it or not, there is someone out there that can do what you do, and probably a lot better than you. This is why God chooses us based on purpose and not skills alone, so never let yourself believe you're in position because you're the only one able to do what you do. It is okay to be confident about what you do, but remain humble. It's also okay for you to know that you're valuable, but it is wise to remind yourself that you're replaceable. Just strive to make God proud and you will have no time to be prideful or big headed.

During your quiet/meditation time, pray and ask God

what your assignment is, and write it down in your notes. If you already know what your assignment is, and there are things that you are fearful or uncomfortable with, write those things down and pray for ways to overcome those fears.

DAY TWENTY-THREE

"Are U Disciplined?"
Today's Scripture: Psalm 37 (Focus v.23-25)

The steps of a good man are ordered by the Lord. Look down at your feet and realize that you didn't get yourself where you are. You might have walked to where you are, but you didn't give yourself the orders to walk there -- God did. You're the vehicle; God is the GPS system navigating every move that you take. You, on this journey, must admit that you are where you are because your steps have been ordered. Every step counts, everything has significance, and every step will somehow land you exactly where you should be even when those steps seem to look unpromising. The place where you currently are is not your final destination, but you are there so that it can prepare you for it.

Although the place in which you stand might be (or is) a painful place, this place still serves great purpose in your life. There are going to be times in your life when you'll go through things that hurt, and you won't understand why you have to hurt, and why the pain has to hurt so terribly. There are even times while on your journey when you may fall, but "falling" doesn't have to mean that it's over for you. Falling down does not equate to failure, choosing to stay down does. If a fall can keep you down and make you believe that you have lost your worth for what you were walking towards, how much faith did you REALLY have in the first place? When you know that you're pressing toward a mark that you deserve, not because you're so good but because God chose you, nothing can separate you from that truth -- not even a bad fall.

There is a prepared place, for a prepared person. What does that mean? It means that your designated place of destiny is waiting for you to arrive and God is ordering your steps to that very place! Can you feel it?!?! Begin to move passionately in that direction.

By now, you have confronted and conquered issues. You have faced the fact that you were chosen for the job. You did your work to ensure that you were not just wanting what God has for you, but also preparing for it one step at a time. So, what now? How do you carry on from here? Well, now, it's time to seriously take what you've learned over these past few weeks and make it applicable to life as you know it presently. This may require you to stay up, or get up, and work when you'd rather be asleep. It may require you to stay in when you'd rather hang out, but in the end, it will be WELL worth it!

Everything that is waiting for you, that you are currently walking and working towards right now, will be well worth it. Not one tear will be wasted. Not one step will be wasted. No energy of effort given will not yield a reward. Every sacrifice and every pain will make sense eventually; maybe not today or tomorrow, but eventually. You will reach a point of revelation and think to yourself, "now I see why it had to happen this way." That thought will sober you and ready you with the faith to trust God on the next journey.

You should pause for a moment of evaluation. Just think about it. Would God watch you prepare for what He has waiting for you, see everything it's costing you to get there, and once you're finally there, it be nothing that is worthwhile? While I'm no expert in theology and doctrine, I know for sure that's contrary to God's character. I also know that God has a plan for you that is full of hope. As a matter of fact, in the scriptures God tells us that He has plans for us that are good and not evil; plans to prosper us. In other words, no matter how tedious the journey becomes, and regardless of the sudden stops, falls, and hurdles along the way -- when it's all said and done, the end result will be that you have prospered; that you were able to claim every good thing that was waiting for you at the conclusion of your journey.

I wouldn't be able to explain what your entire life, journey, and story has been like up until this moment. Every person's steps reflect all different types of suffering. Suffering isn't always an implication of emotional pain. In this context, to suffer simply means to tolerate something; it means to be subjected to something in preparation of an expected conclusion. So, that tells me that everyone's plate is full of SOMETHING. Someone is tolerating being labeled; another person is fighting to ignore opinions circling around their name; and others might be suffering to stay the course. Regardless of the particulars, here's what is true: the sufferings of this present time cannot compare to the glory that will be revealed. And that's why you can't wave the white flag, take a shortcut, or walk away. If you lose your tolerance, you'll forfeit the reward that is being prepared for all of your diligence. Don't you want to be paid for every step taken?

There are two things that you want to keep at the forefront of your mind as you follow God's lead:

1. Don't define your end based on your start, and

2. Don't discredit what will happen because of what has already happened.

Keep walking, your journey continues...

In your notes write down what you are currently going through and how you believe it is preparing you for your better (better you, better place, better relationships, etc.).

DAY TWENTY-FOUR

"U Fix It!"
Today's Scripture: 2 Corinthians 5 (Focus v. 18-19)

We often hear the saying, "if it's not broken, don't try to fix it…". That's cool, I guess, but somehow, somewhere down the line, there was an unspoken rule that became popular, and it says "if you didn't break it, you don't have to fix it.". I don't agree with this in totality whatsoever. I'm sure that the people who use it, have their own justifications that make it work for THEIR situations, but let's be very clear, this doesn't work in ALL situations. Life will teach you that there are some things that will break at no fault of your own, yet you will have the responsibility to mend them. Is that fair? Not necessarily. Is there any benefit to doing so? Almost always.

Sometimes there are shifts and rifts in our human relationships. Things happen. People get hurt and become offended. When this happens, it is typical for "blame" to be placed. When the Blame Game gets going, in most cases, the one you blame is the one you expect to fix it (if it is going to be fixed). BUT, what if the "broken thing" is YOU? Think on that and answer slowly.

When you're the one that has been stabbed, do you sit there and bleed until they feel remorseful enough to remove the knife from your back? That wouldn't be a wise choice because there are some people, no matter how wrong they are, that never admit their wrongs and apologize for their actions. It sucks but that's just some people's nature. You can't allow what someone refuses to do make you neglect what you need to do for yourself and your life. They already left you broken, and now you're going to let them control your healing, too?

Are you going to stay broken because you feel that the same hands that hurt you should be the same hands to heal you? Or will you take the necessary actions to fix "it", to fix you, so that you can move forward? Better yet, why not take a closer look at what happened? Not just from your point of view, but from the point of TRUTH – so that you can see what part YOU played in the breaking?

[insert a pause right here]

Maybe you ignored the warning signs right in your face. Perhaps you ignored God's still small voice telling you to get up and leave while you still had your dignity but instead of listening and leaving, you stayed because you felt strongly that, at some point, in some strange way, hope would come from that hopeless situation. I don't know what part of the bigger picture was painted by you, but you have a part and you need to own it. A part of moving on and healing yourself is being bold enough to accept your actions that added to your brokenness. Fixing won't happen without honesty.

At some point it has to be about what actually matters -

- your healing, peace, and wholeness. If those things are important to you, there should be nothing you wouldn't do to secure them or restore them when they've been lost or damaged -- whether a result of your actions or someone else's. You have to make up in your mind that you want to be fixed and you're no longer willing to wait on anyone -- be it the offender or someone you trust to be a fixer -- to fix you...for you. You have to remember what having true joy felt like before you were damaged, and find a healthy resolution that will navigate you back to that place. This time (and many other times in your future) the fixing is on you. You have total responsibility of your wholeness. Fix what you can and leave the rest to God.

It is impossible that NO offenses should come. If you haven't already, go ahead and accept that truth. By internalizing the truth that you can't escape being wronged by others, it will help you to deal with it on a mature level if it happens. The reason a lot of people are shaken so badly when trauma hits their human relationships is because they've dismissed that as a possibility. Yes, it's true that we should expect the best and do everything in our power to create positive outcomes; however, nobody has the power to control how the details unfold -- especially not in the confines of a relationship. In a relationship, everyone has to be responsible for their own actions. Those actions determine the course of that connection. This is why you should be aware that there is a possibility that offense will happen, maybe not because of anything on your end, but because of someone else's behavior that you cannot control.

You may not be aware of it, but you have the ministry of reconciliation. Reconciliation is the remedy for handling grudges. A grudge is a tool of mental deception. Grudges manipulate your mind into thinking that if you hate them strong enough, long enough, it will heal you eventually or somehow make it all go away or feel better. But that's never how it works out. Bitterness and resentment only poisons the heart that holds it, not the people it's aimed at. I challenge you to loose the grip you have on a grudge. Give your soul permission to be fixed and free. You don't want to continue on your journey and walk into destiny carrying unnecessary weight. Fix it, and FORGIVE!

In your notes write down what needs fixing. However, try to make sure that YOU remain the focus, and not the one who broke what now needs fixing.

DAY TWENTY FIVE

"U Had It All Wrong!"
Today's Scripture: Ephesians 3 (Focus v. 14-19)

The greatest power that we have as humans is the ability to love. The strongest expression of love is when we learn to not only love, but to love unconditionally. To love others without conditions is to love others the way that Christ loves us every single second of the day. It's a deep love embodied with patience and longsuffering. Our souls enjoy everything about love until we taste heartbreak. It doesn't matter who it's from or what happened that broke us, the experience shakes us so violently that we lose our footing on love's foundation, and although we're still alive, we're living without giving, receiving, or even believing in love.

As much as we'd like to be in a world where hearts don't break, feelings don't hurt, and eyes don't cry, the reality is -- pain is inevitable. There's no escape route; there's no perfect world that can shield you from the possibilities of pain. Jesus suffered pain in the name of love; and so will we. The same people that celebrated Him in one moment, supported his crucifixion the next moment; but somehow, Jesus managed to love them and STILL die for them. Jesus knew that in His pain was hidden a treasure of purpose so He had to maneuver through "I've been hurt" (the pain) to get to "it is finished" (the purpose). In this, we find the most raw expression of what unconditional love looks like.

How are you dealing with your letdowns? What kind of person is the pain you're feeling right now transforming you into? The sting of hurt and disappointment that you have been encountering - do you know what it really means?

The sting you've been feeling is not from the initial pain of wrongs done to you at the hands of others. The pain you've been feeling has been from self-inflicted wounds. You have been terrified of letting your guard down and becoming vulnerable because you are afraid that someone will hurt you (again). You promised yourself that you would never feel that kind of pain again if you had any say in it. By all means, you are determined to make sure that the last time was the last time. Every day you wake up with a mind to save yourself from feeling the same pain again.

So, you have been protecting your heart at all costs. You walled yourself in, became spiteful, and unknowingly began to self-destruct. All of this is happening not because it hurts THAT bad but because you've misunderstood your pain. Using the wrong coping strategies is always the result of misunderstanding your pain. What you failed to realize is that the initial pain you felt was not to KILL you, it was actually a "gift" TO you!

I know we struggle to accept GIFTS wrapped in misery and pain, because no one really wants to go through either. However, if you'll just tear away the outside wrapping and open it up, you'll get to see what's inside and understand why it's a gift. It's almost impossible to believe that something not wrapped beautifully can have something beautiful to offer you on the inside. That logic makes sense, but the issue with that is, you have to learn how to judge a gift by the content, not the wrapping alone. Inside of what is wrapped in "misery" is really MINISTRY; and what is wrapped in "pain" is really an expression of PASSION.

Don't live a life full of spite because of what happened. Instead, live a life of LOVE "IN SPITE OF". You had it all wrong, He wasn't teaching you to give up on LOVE – He was teaching you to LOVE others in the same manner in which He loves you. UNCONDITIONALLY!

Be strengthened in your innermost parts. Be rooted and grounded in love, and let no one take that away from you. No one CAN take that away from you. Let nothing separate you from LOVE - "neither height nor depth, nor anything else in all creation, will be able to separate us from the love of God that is in Christ Jesus our Lord." (Romans 8:39)

As you were reading, I am sure at least one relationship came to your mind. In your notes, write down how you can possibly bring it back to a place of unconditional love. Before you get to writing, consider that just because you love someone unconditionally, it doesn't mean that you have to be in their life or they have to be in yours on an intimate level; it means that you have released the hate that would make loving them impossible.

DAY TWENTY-SIX

"Don't U Give Up!"
Today's Scripture: Philippians 3 (Focus v.12-14)

First, stop for a moment and give yourself an applause for making it this far. You are just 4 days away from completing this journey to a better, refined, and more royal version of yourself. How does that make you feel? Accomplished, I hope. For a lot of you, starting was easy and quitting was almost a decision you made at different moments, but something kept you going, something about what the end could reveal intrigued you to the point of remaining persistent. I'm glad that you are still in it to win it because there is surely a prize waiting to be claimed by you at the end of this journey.

No favorable ending happens without intense moments of almost quitting. I am sure, as I said earlier, that some of you may have almost quit at some point; but by being this close to completion, that urge will only become more intense than it's ever been because you are in what is called the "final stretch". The closer you get to being finished, the more everything around you becomes frustrating.

Your job is irritating you; the children are on all of your nerves; and you're thinking about quitting your assignment at the church because it's seemingly more stressful now and not as fulfilling as it once was. My advice to you is: acknowledge what you are feeling but be slow to act on it. Most of what you feel is only an emotional distraction to steer you in the direction of giving up; don't give into it. Make up in your mind that you didn't come this far, invest this much time, or do this much work on yourself to forfeit it all right now.

The Message version for the focus scripture says it this way: *"I'm not saying that I have this all together, that I have it made. But I am well on my way, reaching out for Christ, who has so wondrously reached out for me.*

Friends, don't get me wrong: By no means do I count myself an expert in all of this, but I've got my eye on the goal, where God is beckoning us onward – to Jesus. I'm off and running, and I'm not turning back." (v. 12 –14).

In this scripture, a vivid image of passion and determination is presented. The Apostle Paul makes two things very clear - that he has his eye on the goal and that he is not turning back. At some point, he was met with the realization that while the future was unknown, it was still worth going towards because that's the direction God was pulling him in. We are not any different than Paul. God is pulling us in the direction of His promises for us. Every word spoken concerning you by God will be made alive as you move onward. This is why you can't give up now.

Do you believe in you?

Do you trust that His promises to you are true?

A good practice is to rehearse and repeat every promise from God. Create at least two times of the day where you speak God's word for you back to Him. This will help you find courage on doubtful days, keep you from quitting, and enable you to internalize God's thoughts for you in your heart. If you hide God's word in your heart, it becomes your strength during weak moments and your reason to believe that going on is worth it. Do you know the best part of a hidden word? Nothing or no one has access to it to manipulate, discredit, or change it -- because it's secure and sure.

It's normal to become faint and lose your endurance towards the end of a long race, so don't be alarmed by that. Anyone that is a winner today was weary yesterday. Experiencing fatigue and just being "over it" is an usual part of the fight and journey. Your focus shouldn't be avoiding this but having strategies that work for overcoming it.

You have a few days until the finish line. This is where you should pause for a brief moment, gather yourself, and find your second wind to go the rest of the distance. Stop and stretch if you must. Stop and pray if that will give you a boost of energy. Whatever you do, I charge you to NOT stop and quit. You are so worth this win. Take it step by step, day by day. Don't let your mind get stuck in temporary places. PRESS!!! Move forward to where God is taking you! Don't let fatigue become a distraction – keep going!!

In your notes, write down where you were -- mentally, emotionally, spiritually, physically -- at the start of this journey. Then, write down where you are now in each of those areas. Compare each list to one another and note your growth. You'll probably discover that you have made more advancements than you were aware of.

DAY TWENTY-SEVEN

"It's Got to Mean Something to U"
Today's Scripture: 2 Peter 1 (Focus v. 10)

In this focus scripture, the writer admonishes us to do something that I believe is extremely important. It says: *[YOU] make your call and election sure, for if you do these things you will never stumble:" (v.10).* We are told that if we make our call and election sure, we will never stumble. In other words, it has to mean something to YOU! That is the nugget for us to chew on here. That everything we do-- dreams, passions, goals, changes, and the like--has to mean something to us. In our heart and mind, there should be a definition that places a deep meaning on the things that we have been called and elected to do.

Don't let other people want more for you than you want for yourself. When people want it for you more than you want it for yourself, your every move will be inspired by their opinions or thoughts about what you should be doing and how you should be doing it. Or, much worse, you won't move much or at all simply because your call and election is not sure within you. Anything that is not sure within you can be easily manipulated by outside sources. Anytime you place your passion and purpose for life in the hands of someone else, you give them power over you, and you position yourself to be a puppet of sorts.

On the other hand, maybe you are sure of your calling and election. Maybe you are someone without any doubts about what you were put here to do and what is in your heart to give for a chance at seeing the world around you become better. Yet, you fear change although your call and election is sure. It is your fear of change that has you crippled (or will if it hasn't already) and made your life come to a standstill when you should really be moving forward. If that's your story, I want to submit to you that, change comes with the package; don't fear it, let it happen. Don't get caught up in trying to determine the "if" or "maybe" factors of it all. Leave that to God. The unknown details are better left to the author and finisher of your faith. When you give yourself to the process of changing, God will give grace for the unknown details. In knowing this, we can gain the courage to trust the Lord with all of our hearts knowing that He promises to direct our paths.

In the words of my Bishop, Bishop William H. Murphy, III, in order to change, you've got to go through some CHANGES! Changes are designed eerily similar to roller coasters - they come with high points, dips in the middle, and frightful lows that happen before you have time to brace yourself. You can't customize the ride to fit what you can handle or what you prefer. Either you are going to accept the ride as it is or you can make the choice not to ride it--and so is the case with changes. If you are not willing to deal with the changes of change, you may need to stay off the ride.

What are those changes? There are variations; it's different for every person. They can range from changes in personal convictions to changes in your emotional state; changes in how you view your passion and purpose in the earth and changes in how you communicate with others around you.

Change is a choice that you make because you deem it important to you. If change is about benefiting others, it's not really change, it's an appeal to please people. The difference between a person that changes for themselves and a person that changes for others is how concerned they are about what someone else thinks of their decisions and process. When it matters to you, it doesn't have to matter to anyone else. Why? Because you are settled and sure about why you are changing, what the purpose of your change is, and most importantly, what God is trying to accomplish in you.

Are you tired of going around the same mountain(s)?

Do you want better for your life?

Are you dedicated to your dreams and vision?

If someone else ALWAYS has to push you to do something that you say you're passionate about, perhaps you need an additional "30 days". If you lack the zeal to do what you are supposed to be sure of, you're not as sure as you might have convinced yourself that you are. When you are sure, your actions reflect that. When you are sure, every effort and endeavor begins with you. Indeed, others may push and support you along the way, but even if they don't, you should still be on course with your assignment.

In your notes section, write down what your passion, purpose, and assignment mean to you. What you are called to do has to mean something to YOU! Don't pass this point without discovering that meaning.

DAY TWENTY-EIGHT

"The SON Is Shining On U!"
Today's Scripture: Deuteronomy 28 (Focus v. 8)

In the focus scripture for today, we are told that the Lord will command a blessing in our storehouses. It doesn't stop there, though. After the Lord commands a blessing in our storehouses, He will then bless us in the land that He is giving us. These are 2 key points that are essential to our journeys even beyond this present 30 Day Royal Makeover that we are on.

So often we misappropriate our focus and our diligence. We misappropriate our focus by paying attention to what's happening in the storehouses around ours, not realizing that we are neglecting the one that God has given to us to work and be faithful over. As a result, our diligence suffers severely. When our focus is lost and our diligence is out of place, we monitor the undertakings of the next person. What are they doing? How well are they doing it?

There are things that we love to do, and then, there are things that we are anointed to do in the earth. When those two worlds collide, the outcome is life-changing! However, we must be sure that we are focusing on what is in our storehouses, and not what's in our neighbors' storehouses. You can't be jealous over what someone else has going on; that's their grace -- it is up to you to work yours! What happens and what you have in YOUR storehouse is a direct result of the grace that God has stamped on YOUR life. Realize what that grace is and work it diligently until increase, promotion, and more is granted to you. Realize that the SON is shining on you and in your storehouse.

Pastor Tasha Cobbs said it this way: "Find who you are, and what you do, and stick with it until God puts the blessing on it..." This is a very simple formula to never miss what God has for you...right where you are. In a haste to get to the next big thing or do whatever we believe will bring us a sense of accomplishment, we tend to overlook all that is already in motion and all that already belongs to us. You don't have to create your next moment or forge a new path. Why? God has plans to GIVE you land. The possibilities of what that "land" will be for you are limitless. It can be anything from a new job, career and ministry advancements, a spouse that loves you in a way you never fathomed, and so on. The best part about it is, this "land" God is going to bless you with will be yours exclusively. There will be no need to fight to get or maintain it, compete with anyone around you, or downplay your gifts and anointing in exchange for opportunities or acceptance.

Be diligent and faithful in your work and He will cause the SON to shine upon you! There are very specific things that the Earth is waiting on that only your storehouse can produce. That book, that outreach ministry, your testimony, your gift, your anointing. What you have been trusted to do has the ability to change culture, make a difference, and impact the lives of people around you. And it starts with using the SON that's shining on you to light up the environment around you.

In your notes, write down what is in your "storehouse". Write down what you should be doing to maximize what you have and then create ways to live on the highest level according to the potential and grace that's been stamped on your life by God.

DAY TWENTY-NINE

"The Unstoppable U!"
Today's Scripture: 1 Corinthians 9 (Focus v. 24)

In the focus scripture for today, it talks about running a race. The scripture informs us that everyone in the race runs but only one person wins the prize. In the latter clause of this scripture, it admonishes us to run in a way that we might receive the prize that is available at the end of the race. There's a truth found here that we should all be able to accept which is: just because everyone won't win the race doesn't mean that everyone shouldn't run as if they want to or can win the race. That established, I want to ask you: how are you running?

Are you running just to run?

Are you running as if you are unstoppable?

Are you running in a way that reveals your desire to actually win the race?

Whether you know it or not, it matters how you run. You have to know that it matters that you approach every race with an unstoppable mindset. Will that always mean winning? No. There will be some unwon races. However, if you run with an unstoppable mindset, you will always keep your mobility; and that is what you will need at all times on any journey that you find yourself on. As long as you believe in your mind that you are unstoppable, nothing -- not even the most arduous challenges -- can convince you otherwise. From your determination to be unstoppable (steadfast, not easily moved, resilient, strong-willed), the ability to be mobile is created. You only have one more day left in this journey, but even after Day 30, you must make the choice to remain "MOBILE".

What does it mean to be mobile? Mobility is defined as the movement of people in a population, as from place to place, from job to job, or from one social class or level to another. In the context of this 30 Day Makeover, I am confident that you have experienced some movement in the said areas, as well as other areas that are more spiritually centered, and even in areas that are more personal. With this in mind, you get a very clear realization as to what the benefits of remaining mobile are right now and can be in the future. By remaining mobile, it is impossible for your life to reach a standstill in any area. Your growth will last as long as you are unstoppable. If you refuse to give up or give in, you welcome continued success into your life and you make room for the evolution of your unrealized royalty. There are just too many benefits of being mobile to allow anything that seems like a good reason to quit to actually make you quit.

What does your mobility feel like now compared to 29 days ago? It should be a lot easier to move forward. Moving forward should come as second nature to you; it should be something that you now do by instinct and not out of obligation. Yes? You're not just another somebody running this race. Now, at this very moment, you are unstoppable and you possess the kind of mobility with great fortitude that will fuel your ability to run onward. It is these qualities that will set the distinction between you and anyone else.

It's Day 29! If nothing has stopped you by now, don't allow anything to stop you between now and the moment when you'll stride across the finish line on Day 30. In fact, don't let anything make you stop even when THIS particular race ends. You might have lacked endurance prior to this makeover, but you have it now. It's embedded in who you are, it's a brand new piece of your identity. Being unstoppable will never mean that rough points will be inescapable. It does not even mean that you won't need to stop in order to regroup yourself and catch your breath. It just means, instead, that you won't surrender and exit the race altogether. As you go on, try to always remember: the intention of being unstoppable is not the avoidance of stopping; the intention is to never stop moving forward.

You can get ready to RUN!! No chains!!! No limits!!! God has broken the chains and removed the limits off of your mobility. Run with the freedom that comes along with being the UNSTOPPABLE you! The "U" that you were before this point in time was someone that wrestled with bondage and suffered from things that impeded your capability of being mobile, future oriented, and forward minded. That version of yourself that you faced in your yesterdays, you will see no more in your future -- unless you allow them back into your life.

In your notes, write down the things that were once hard for you to move on from, and what you do now in order to move forward that you couldn't do before.

DAY THIRTY

"The Better U!"
Today's Scripture: Ephesians 4 (Focus v.22-24)

Welcome to the end of THIS PORTION of your journey!!!!! Why just "this portion"? Because your journey is defined as a traveling from one place to another, usually taking a rather long time. So, you're not done, you're just gearing up to go to another place. Remember, it's all about mobility and being unstoppable. While this segment of the trip is over and completed, there is still more to do beyond this point. More work, more assignments, more outreach, more lighting the world with your light, more operating as royalty. Every ending is a brand new beginning. Each time you arrive at one destination, a journey to a new one begins. Now that you have stepped into the BETTER U, the former you has no more relevance or power. All things are made new.

You don't want to feel as if you have completely ARRIVED, because that leaves no room for your continued growth and maturity. You want to move forward from "this place" and go to another level of greatness... to another level of BETTER! Your destiny calls for it! An easy way to become a roadblock on your own path to destiny is by feeling like just because you have finished this juncture of your journey, you have arrived and you now know it all and there is nothing more to strive for personally and spiritually. Don't let that become your attitude. Instead, acknowledge that you don't know it all, that there is more for you to experience, and that there is a great deal of information and wisdom for you to obtain as you step into a new level of life. An attitude that says "there's more" creates the hunger to pursue it and the humility to have it.

Finishing this makeover doesn't mean the end of challenges for you whatsoever, but it does mean that you can now handle them with deeper insight and greater fortitude. Trouble can't throw you off course when you're armed with the right tools to confront and conquer whatever comes your way. The difference between who you were then and who you are now is that you are prepared. You are prepared with a better sense of self and God; you are prepared with insight on how to balance life and your crown; and you are prepared with a fresher perspective on life and your unique, one-of-a-kind, purpose in life. Since you are prepared, you can't lose at what YOU were created for on earth. Preparation is protection against losing your royal assignment and purpose.

I am SO PROUD of the new, and improved, YOU! You didn't simply wake up one morning and discover this new person that you didn't know the day before. You worked diligently to become this new version of yourself. On the days when committing to this makeover became gruesome and unbearable, you found strength that you didn't know existed on the inside of you and used it to persevere. You could have walked away from it all each time people turned their backs and opened their mouths to talk down at you about your journey. They might have said things like, "*Oh, you're doing too much. Who do you think you are?*" But what did you do? You decided that where you were headed was far greater and more important than anything that was being said about you. For these reasons and so many more, I couldn't be more happy for you and proud of your accomplishment.

As you move on beyond this point, I want to challenge you to keep today's focus scripture in mind, which reads: You were taught, with regard to your former way of life, to put off your old self, which is being corrupted by its deceitful desires; to be made new in the attitude of your minds; and to put on the new self, created to be like God in true righteousness and holiness. (v. 22-24)

WELCOME TO BETTER!

ABOUT THE AUTHOR

Shanicka Vail House has a huge heart for youth and young adults, but in that has a strong passion for young girls and women. From that passion came the inception of "be.UteeQUEEN", a mentorship program under the umbrella of "ANCHOREDroyalty", whose purpose is to teach and train young girls and women how to discover the royalty they were created in. The be.UteeQUEENS, worldwide, live by a golden rule: "never let your crown fall". On June 1, 2014 Shanicka released her first children's book geared towards young girls entitled, "The "i" Inside of ME". This is a book of affirmations that connects each "Princess" with the greatness inside of her.

Shanicka is humbled to serve and assist others in many different capacities. She prays that these books will be tools in the hand of every reader, used to groom each of them into greater servants with a willingness to aid in building others and ultimately building The Kingdom!

Made in the USA
Lexington, KY
13 May 2015